THE Paris Journal

BOOK I

EVAN ROBERTSON & NICHOLE ROBERTSON

OBVIOUS STATE

© 2014 Obvious State

Written by Evan Robertson and Nichole Robertson
Photographs by Nichole Robertson
Published by Obvious State

ISBN 978-1-63330-001-9

Creative Director, Evan Robertson
Art Director, Marissa Rivera
Editor, Amy Feezor

Obvious State
New York + Paris
www.obviousstate.com

zero

TO THE ESCAPE ARTISTS

6:35 AM

Cité
METRO

CITÉ

Mode d'emploi

Paris

THE TRAIN LIGHTS FLICKER OUT AS WE MAKE A SLOW, WIDE ARC TOWARD THE CITÉ METRO STATION IN THE HEART OF PARIS.

An impulse rises up from the waves of sleepiness: we're here. I grab my backpack and stand as soon as there is enough light to make out the details of the cabin. My head is giddy and indifferent to the jet lag in my arms and legs. It floats like a balloon pulling a heavy ribbon, dragging the rest of me though the rocking car toward the doors.

I take a deep breath of the tunnel air and imagine the breezy streets above me. I won't write "ah, Paris," but I feel it. This isn't my first time here, just my first time in too long.

I step over the careless leg of a girl sleeping on her boyfriend. He's smiling. And smiling is practically dancing in the aisles for Parisians. Somebody must have gotten lucky last night. Her brown hair is a little frizzy; it's damp today. But it's often damp here, and bad hair is just the price you pay.

I move through the aisle with the slowing train, pulled by the momentum past the only other person: an older man sitting alone. He glances up from his newspaper. I glance back. He's handsome, unshaven in a good way, and somehow pulling off a pair of pointy shoes. Well done.

I know what you're thinking. Please don't play matchmaker. I won't be resting my frizzy hair on anyone's shoulder.

My heart belongs to Paris.

The train is directly under the river now, where the metro line crosses the Seine like a giant X-marks-the-spot. A treasure map for explorers! Love for the lucky! Enlightenment for believers!

And crêpes for everyone else.

I reach the metro door and check my watch. About 10 minutes left. I grab the handle and claim first position to leave. No matter your age, there's a childish thrill in beating everyone to the exit.

I hear Frizzy Hair laugh behind me. She and Got Lucky are heading for the other door. They stumble against the momentum of the train, and she feigns a fall into him. Player.

His luck holds up because he keeps his balance. They glance at me as she whispers in his ear. He lifts his metro door handle up and to the left, and then holds it there. A clear challenge.

If it's a race you want, it's a race you'll get.

Lights on. The train glides into the bright semi-dome of the station then curves to a halt. Both doors pop open. Already in motion, I step onto the platform as Lucky and Frizz lose their balance this time and stumble backward. Disaster at the gate!

I look for the stairs, but am distracted by the long, orderly line of silver lamps. Each post rises and curves like a spent lily, drooping down into three glowing orbs. Together, they flood the cavernous white-tiled arch of the ceiling with a light so endlessly reflected, it feels sourceless.

When I come to, Frizz and Lucky are already at the stairs. The steps zigzag back and forth across the massive cistern that leads to the surface 20 meters above. Too late to catch them, I gamble on a different route.

The riveted metal walls gleam like the skin of a 19th-century diving bell. And like divers, my competitors have to take a break halfway up - in this case, to make out.

Suckers. I jump in the elevator behind the older man just as the doors close, and we begin our quick ascent to the station entrance.

I win, and the day is mine.

7:15 AM

Pont
LOUIS-
Phillipe

UNLIKE NEW YORK, PARIS IS THE CITY THAT SLEEPS.

No matter how early you wake up in New York, you've already missed it. Someone was up earlier. Something already happened. Someone else caught the worm.

But here, a long silence reigns from about 2:00am until dawn. Then, when the sun rises, you have the pleasure of waking up with everyone else. Notable exceptions: Me, bakers, and drunk twenty-something Brits.

My head aches from the jet lag and lack of sleep, but the cool damp air helps. I'm here to watch the city wake up. Like a creepy, stalky girlfriend, I want to watch it open its eyes. Good morning, lover. Whatcha thinking about?

I walk toward the Pont Saint-Louis, glancing around for the first sign of people. None, so I jog. The light show is about to begin. The cloudless sky grows brighter by the minute, then the sun emerges from behind the rooftops along the right bank. To the south, the light grazes the roofs of the tallest Haussmann buildings on the Île Saint-Louis. It slowly creeps down the dormer windows set out from the mansard roofs, then down further to the balconies. Elaborate, lacy shadows gain definition and dance between the intricate stonework and wrought iron.

The sunrise has already claimed two full rows of windows. They reflect light onto the entire length of the bridge, and a tall double window near the edge of the building casts a fiery orange onto me. Behind that double window, someone feels the warmth on his eyelids. Rise and shine! The Sun King calls! Time for your morning ablutions! Time to saunter down the boulevards!

The light drips like white paint down the stone facade, reaching the second floor, where a man opens his window to let it in. He peeks out from behind an impressive gray mustache to assess the weather. He squints down-river, then toward the street below where a petite woman sees him and waves good morning. Wife? Neighbor?

Definitely mistress.

When the sunlight finally reaches the water, it gilds the reflection of the buildings and trees with gold. The water sparkles as it flows under the bridge, then bounces the light onto its stone underbelly. In a few minutes, the sun will rise high enough to reach over the tops of the right bank buildings, and will dress the streets in a uniform of pale yellow. But in these last few moments, everything is orange and pink and ephemeral. It illuminates the island like a hall of natural mirrors.

A moped roars by, straining second gear. Somewhere in the interior of the island, a dog barks, and a woman barks back. The spell is broken, and Monsieur Moustache is down on the street now, waiting for his dog to sniff a tangle of grass. The day is bright and full of possibility. And here I am standing still.

Time to go.

CAFÉ
Saint-Régis

Petit Déjeuner   7€
- 1 boisson chaude
- 1 croissant ou 1 tartine
- 1 jus d'orange pressée

FORMULE COUP DE CŒUR   11€
- 1 boisson chaude
- 1 viennoiserie
- Pain bio Moisangrillé, beurre échiré
- 2 confitures
- 1 jus d'orange pressée
- 1 œuf à la coque

RUE JEAN DU BELLAY RUNS DIRECTLY INTO THE BRIDGE THAT CONNECTS THE TWO ISLANDS, PONT SAINT-LOUIS.

Outside of Café Saint-Régis, which faces the bridge from the Saint-Louis side, the staff prepares for the morning customers. It's chillier here. The sun won't reach the interior of the island for hours. The only warmth emanates from inside the café, carrying good smells with it. A waitress, clearly in charge, directs the staff as she organizes the one-shot cups on top of the espresso machine.

The two waiters drag tipsy stacks of cane chairs to the sidewalk. There's very little street traffic on the island, but on its perimeter, the sound of cars and mopeds steadily builds. Morning has arrived, and everyone moves quickly now.

The waitress comments on the cold as she readies the tables with ashtrays and menus for the earliest guests. She heads back in with her empty tray, passing one of the waiters who is carrying salt, pepper and sugar. She returns with a tray of vases, each with one small red carnation.

Where did the second waiter sneak off to? There. He has rounded the corner and lit up a cigarette. Rough night. With one foot against the wall he takes a long drag. I wonder what kept him up all night. Insomnia? Tolstoy? No, a breakup. Crazy Pauline again with her possessiveness and drunk dialing.

If only he knew how much the waitress digs him, but he can't see it. She waits, just inside, with her back to him - an obvious ploy. Feigned indifference. Look how she pulls a shot from the shiny espresso machine. Look how she sips that shot as if it weren't a metaphor for something else.

The games we play.

Across the street at another café, a potbellied man in a blue sweater hands a broom to the bus boy. He gestures to some trash in the street, and walks back toward the restaurant. The bus boy sweeps last night's cigarettes into the gutter along with the remnants of a baguette. The food attracts a flock of pigeons. To get rid of them, he flicks a piece of bread in their direction, startling and delighting them all at once. The rhythmic scrape of the broom blends with the sounds of flapping wings as they approach again. He sends another piece flying, which sends the pigeons flying.

Up the street, a large green sanitation truck blasts the sidewalks clean as the washing outlets in the gutter turn on. The deluge sends even the feistiest pigeons to the balconies. But they'll be back for breakfast. The last of the water snakes its way down the gutters taking everything with it, leaving behind the scent of fresh rain on the pavement.

Back at Café Saint-Régis, the eight chairs and four tables are filling up now. Customers settle in as the wait staff picks up the tempo. The two waiters rush back and forth, in and out of the doors, greeting each guest and passing out menus. Just above the flurry of activity, an apartment window over the café opens and a lanky man leans on the windowsill to smoke a cigarette. He looks down, nods to one of the waiters, then idly stares at the action unfolding on the street.

He barely smokes. The cigarette is only a timer, and the street is his therapy. From up there, he can see it all - the cafés, the patrons, the pigeons, the food and menus and drinks - for what it is: a ritual. Routines wear you down and dull your senses. But rituals connect. You to yourself, you to everyone else. No one here has grabbed a croissant and coffee to eat on the run. They sit. They linger. And whether they know it or not, they're a part of something bigger and wonderful. It's simple, human and holy.

A table opens up and I take my seat. I'll order a coffee and drink it to wake up. But that's not why I'm here. I'm here to be here. I'm here to be part of it. To watch the ritual unfold. To take part in doing nothing.

And maybe that Crazy Pauline will show. Now that would be something.

9:00 AM

Notre
DAME

IT'S CHILLY. I ASK FOR THE CHECK.

I'm disappointed in my American restlessness, but I can't sit still any longer. Besides, thinking about rituals has given me a much better idea. I decide to go to Notre Dame this morning before it's sacked by tourists. Right now, it will be as empty as Jacob's kettle. That's a bible reference. See how I did that?

I pay the check and head across the Pont Saint-Louis toward Notre Dame Cathedral.

I am not a particularly religious person, but I come here each time I'm in Paris. Entering the church feels like stepping into another place and time, and the transition from the outside hits every one of your senses. Outside, the sun floods the large square with light; inside, light is restricted and organized. It filters through the opulent windows, and huddles in concentric rings of votive candles.

Noises outside are loud and staccato; within, they are hushed and reverberant. The faded smells of old incense hang in the still air. All five senses reach out to the space, and the space, soaring 30 meters above you, reaches back.

In this moment, you could tell me God is a spatula and I would believe you.

Above me, the vaulted arches direct my eyes up. On the street, we ignore the vast space above us. But Notre Dame creates a contradiction - the interior is light and airy, yet the structure around it is heavy and massive. The height of it makes me feel dizzy and small. If you can accept that the geometric stone ceiling can float up there without crushing you, then maybe something else can as well, something more beautiful and perfect in its geometry.

Seeing is believing. And every time I see this, for a brief moment, I believe.

This church, completed almost 700 years ago, still has its own parish of worshippers. On a busy day, it feels like a circus. But even then, the parishioners of Notre Dame come here to worship and manage to tune out the buzzing flies. Only a few of the faithful are here today. They are lost in thought and prayer. They sit in the pews and gaze at statues in the galleries.

As I walk the perimeter of the church, an organist practices a hymn. I follow at a distance behind a small group of Japanese tourists, who are slowly pacing the side aisle to admire the windows and galleries. We circle the dedicated congregation in the center nave.

I come to Paris to escape the noise. But here, in this moment, I am the noise. We are the noise. We parade around while the real attendants sing a hymn, while the priest pours the blessed water, and while an old lady prays to the Virgin Mary. They're oblivious to us.

A tour bus empties new visitors into the side aisles, and suddenly the quiet hiss of the dormant organ pipes is overrun with rustling backpacks, clicking cameras, exclamations and coughs. Despite the distractions of the uncomprehending audience, the congregation remains focused on their ritual.

And what about me? Should I submit as well? Submit to whatever is up there high above the ceiling with impossible geometry? I think about it for a moment. But in the church of my own mind, a thousand distractions gather: responsibilities, chores, instant messages, viral videos, voicemail, email, junk mail. They distract my old, slow, faithful thoughts from their duty.

I open the exit door and step into the jarring light of the outside world.

9:45 AM

PONT de l'Archevêché

I MAKE MY WAY AROUND THE SIDE OF NOTRE DAME.

The charming path between the Seine and the cathedral provides the best view of its flying buttresses. Grand, ornate and a little odd, they are like distinguished scars. They're not flaws, they're features. Like Marilyn Monroe's mole or Bob Dylan's voice.

And they're just the tip of the iceberg. Any city as old as Paris has tons of once-warty features. But with time, they become essential to its identity. I love them all. The Centre Pompidou. The Moulin Rouge. Even the Eiffel Tower sometimes. But as I round the corner behind the church, I come face to face with the one disfigurement I cannot accept, no matter how hard I try: The love locks. Our Lady help me, the love locks, shackled to the "love" bridge.

You see, long ago, under the cover of night, two lovers scratched their initials on a lock and slapped it onto this bridge's fence. They tossed the key into the river, kissed with tongue, then ran hard from the police. High on the adrenaline rush of sticking it to The Man, they fled under a bridge and promptly stuck it to each other. I suppose at one time this act of protest had a romantic air. Lovers imagined themselves as standing up for something worthwhile in the face of some repressive force. A modern-day Romeo and Juliet defying the rules in the name of love. "Hear ye, O Montagues, O Capulets! Here do we chain ourselves to this good cause. Love is the only rule!"

Except it isn't Romeo and Juliet chained to the bridge: It's their rusty bike lock.

Looking around for the agents of oppression, and there aren't any, they scrawl their initials on there: RM + JC. No threatening prince. No protesting families. Just a bunch of people snapping locks on a bridge all day.

Face it: The Man don't care, ma chérie. He's not pounding the pavement looking for lock bandits. He's not lurking in the bushes. There is no covert sting operation, just tourists standing in a disorganized line, locks in hand, looking in vain for a clean spot on the wire grate to click it shut. Maybe on top of this lock here? Or along that big bike chain sticking out? What do you think, honey? Forget the wild abandon under the bridge, let's just get this over with, snap a photo and be done with it. Strictly hookup insurance.

I don't enjoy feeling cynical about it. I reassure myself that underneath all the half-hearted gestures and lukewarm sentiments, there may be a few locks placed by the genuinely smitten. And buried deep under the locks chained to locks chained to locks, under the derivatives of a derivative of a sentiment, under the metastasized metal masses that literally reach out into the street to bust shins and frighten small children, underneath it all lies that original lock placed by the original crazy-in-love couple.

But I'll never know which one is theirs.

10:30 AM

le Marché AUX *FLEURS*

LEAVING THE LOVE LOCKS BEHIND, I HEAD BACK TOWARD THE INTERIOR OF THE ISLAND.

I cut across Rue de la Cité, past the metro stop, when I stumble into a horrible trap: I smell the flowers.

Like a mindless drone bee, I veer off course and toward Hennion Alley— the venus flytrap of Paris. The heady smell of the freesia and hyacinth lures me into the alleyway, triggering a hopeless fantasy of bright blooms in crystal vases and potted perennials by open windows. All of this happening, presumably, in some apartment I will never own, and attended to by some man servant I will never be able to pay.

Even if I only get the four-day roses, I will promptly kill them. I don't want them dead; I just can't help it. Have you read *Of Mice and Men*? I'm the Lennie of gardening: "They're just so cute, and I wanted them roses so bad, so I watered them, and petted them, until I done broke them."

I remember this most of the time, but conveniently forget it when I smell them. Even the paltriest flower shop has a mind-wiping effect on me. This particular flower market has cost me dearly in the past. The seductive scents and soft petals zombify my senses. My wallet comes out and … wham! The trap springs. Before I know it, I've spent 50 euros on a potted citrus tree that will wither in an empty rental apartment come Thursday.

How is this possible, you wonder? What nitwit buys a garden plant on vacation? This girl, right here. I am the perfect mark for flower pimps. I call them pimps because of their callous disregard for the safety of flowers. After all, if they truly cared about them, they wouldn't sell them to me.

I beeline toward the white jasmine when she steps out of nowhere: a squat little lady with wild hair and enormous boobs. Definitely a Flower Pimp. I miss what she says, but her eyes say "cash or credit?" There's no foreplay in this place.

Now your average shop owner will chat about the weather to get things started. Even the pharmacists politely ask if you need help. But these Flower Pimps cut right to the chase:

"Hot willing flower. 38 euros. You pay now, then do whatever you want with it."

Buy the sweet jasmine, I whisper to myself. I won't have to get it home on the plane because I'm going to kill it anyway.

The shock of this death-cult thinking brings me down from the flower high. I politely turn her down and walk away.

I must have accidentally sniffed some poppies because I swear to God, the woman teleports from behind and reappears in front of me. When I turn around, you know, looking for the wormhole or demon-maw she must have stepped through, I see her right where I left her by the jasmine. OMG, she's a replicant! She murmurs out of the side of her mouth to a third replicant stepping out from behind a mirror.

Compared to death by replicant horde, 38 euros suddenly seems cheap.

Then I notice the subtle differences. The different clogs. Different frocks. Different moles. After decades of pimping the same street, these three women have merged into one omnipresent being. Flower Pimp Two walks toward me, as I back up with a dumb smile. One and Three guard their plant. Sensing my weakness, Flower Pimp Two gestures to the hyacinth.

I reach for my wallet.

But before I take it out, a group of clouds move in, and I suddenly see the flowers in a different light. I wonder how they ended up working for the Flower Pimps. Broken homes? A rocky start? Indentured servitude? If I bought them and treated them to my usual plant care regimen, wouldn't it be a mercy killing?

I make an awkward exit and run.

11:45 AM

PLACE
Dauphine

THERE'S A PLEASANT, NARCOTIC-FREE BREEZE BACK OUT ON THE OPEN STREET.

It clears away the pollen - and pressure - that hung in the air of the alleyway. I check to verify I'm not carrying any stowaway flowers, and head toward the tip of the island. It's late morning, and even the laziest late-risers are out now. On the busy streets, tourists and locals alike spill off the sidewalks into the traffic. A few Italians have a close brush with a bus, but they barely flinch. Italians aren't easily fazed.

A few clear rays of sun tantalize the crowds, and give me the brilliant idea of walking by the water and doing absolutely nothing.

I cut across the square toward the massive gold-leafed gate of the Palais de Justice and to the left, away from the Conciergerie. To tell the truth, the Conciergerie freaks me out a bit. Something about Marie Antoinette sitting alone in her dank cell waiting for the revolutionaries to get around to chopping her head off.

On a sunny stroll, it's easy to tune out the long, violent history of Paris. I'm not just talking about plants I've killed. I mean mayhem. The Revolution. The Terror. The bloggers at Paris Fashion Week.

The scattered rays reach a pair of ducks on the wall by the Seine. I give them my best French "quack," but apparently my accent is poor because they just stare at me. They should at least give me points for trying to speak their language.

While maintaining my stare-down with the Gaulish ducks, I step back into the street. The light changes against me, and a squadron of mopeds charge like dragoons. I bolt for my life.

Shaken by the surprise attack, I retreat to a side street, Rue de Harlay, where the traffic is less militant. The roar of mopeds diminishes until I can hear the wind again. I head up a footpath of pale cobblestones to the tranquil Place Dauphine.

At the other end, the buildings on either side narrow to a gentle point toward the tip of the island. Funny how despite its triangular shape, we still call this a square. There's nothing particularly remarkable about Place Dauphine, which is why I love it. Without a compelling reason for visitors to come, people gather here to meet and to linger. That's all. And that's enough.

Today, it's a group of four men playing bocce. The tallest one tosses the jack into the playing field. His teammate, at least 80 with a long aquiline nose and a permanent grin, tosses the first ball. He knocks the jack with ease.

The noise attracts the attention of a small dog on the other side of the "square." He stares at the bocce balls with his back to his female owner. She looks about 50, and I hope I look half as hot as her when I'm that age. She calls to the pooch in singsongy tones - "oooooh!" - and waves his own soggy ball for him. He doesn't go for it. He's got a new ball. A better ball!

He charges at the men like Napoleon at the Prussians. The speed is amazing, relative to his comically short legs. He kicks up dirt behind him, and scoops up the tall man's perfectly arced ball just before it reaches the jack. The men howl in disgust as little Napoleon tears in a wide, triumphant victory lap around the square.

"I claim this yummy ball in the name of France!"

The men wheel around, all piss and vinegar and white hair on end, looking for a head to put on a pike. The hottie rushes right up to the four men, her laugh just ahead of her. She smiles through an apology with one hand on a curvy hip. The wails of indignation die down to unsure mumbles. She presses on with a gesture to the sun and a comment about the unseasonably warm afternoon.

At the farthest point of the triangular square, Napoleon has put down the heavy ball and is staring up at a second floor window. He is dead still except for the frantic wagging of his tail. From the high window, another dog looks back.

"Josephine! Light of my life, fire of my missing loins!"

Meanwhile, the flirtations have melted the men into laughter. I don't know what the woman just said, but the old man's perma-grin has grown. The second pair of men retrieve the abandoned ball and wish the lady, and little Napoleon, a good day. The woman and her dog leave the men in possession of the square again. Josephine, imprisoned like a monarch, must be content to watch the world below pass her by. Maybe she keeps a journal, too.

A couple in one of the cafés is sharing a croque-monsieur. No, it doesn't make me feel alone. It makes me hungry. I'm going back over to La Ferme Saint-Aubin for some of the most decadent cheeses imaginable and a well-baked baguette.

Then, I'm going to have a picnic with the King of France.

12:30 PM

RUE
chanoinesse

NOTHING MAKES ME WALK WITH PURPOSE LIKE A GOOD CHEESE RUN.

I dodge onto the side streets where I can stretch my legs. The route is longer, but the walk is more pleasant, which is always the best choice. I turn the corner onto Rue Chanoinesse. That's when I see the new store.

"Le Cupcakes." A big sign. Without a hint of irony. Le friggin' cupcakes.

Let's get something straight: I didn't come here for cupcakes. I came here for the finer things: challenging cheeses, game meats, complex sauces. I refuse to spoil my appetite with a cupcake intended for Americans on vacation. Never mind that I am one, I just don't want to be perceived as one. I may not have mastered French, but I have most certainly mastered the French pout. I'm practically an honorary Gaul.

Vive la résistance!

Je suis Sainte Geneviève!

I steel myself against the cultural onslaught of the invaders. Down with Starbucks! Down with Micky D's and KFC. And down with cupcakes!

I march into the tiny shop, and face a fierce row of pink cupcakes lined up like a Mary Kay firing squad. The friendly French girl (French?) behind the counter hands a pair of cupcakes to a Parisian couple (Parisian??). Being locals, they don't have to worry about looking like locals. They get to enjoy the cupcakes without any self-loathing. They just smile and go, taking my resolve with them. The girl asks if she can help me.

I buy two. It's a long walk.

There aren't any cars or pedestrians on the side streets of this part of the island. It feels like pre-dawn Paris again. I can imagine the city in any century. Naturally, I pick late 19th and stroll down the middle of the empty street.

A priest in his robe rounds the corner ahead with a large stack of music papers. The faint noise of a piano emanates from the basement of one of the four-story buildings that hover over the tiny street. A rehearsal for a Sunday recital? As I approach the stone wall at the end of the street, I see the outline of a graffiti poster that has discolored the stones. It leaves a dark impression in the form of a human figure. The music from the rehearsal crescendos, giving the ghostly shape a sense of intention.

It's the ghost of Claude Debussy, here to admonish my utterly un-French choice of snack.

What a snob. This cupcake is good, Claude. Besides, I hear cupcakes are all the rage this year.

I stroll toward the wall as the piano player shifts from forte to fortissimo. That's when the bicyclist veers around the corner heading straight at me. His brakes and I squeal in unison as I dash to the sidewalk. The bicyclist lets out a short stupid laugh and keeps going. His stupid yellow backpack sloshes around with its stupid belongings.

Then I see it: the remains of my cupcake, broken in the gutter. Impaled by a cigarette butt. I desperately calculate how much of it might still be edible. I look up at the smug shadow of Debussy on the wall. My misfortune is his entertainment.

But then I remember the second cake. The safety cake. I knew I bought two for a reason. Not so dumb, am I, Claude?

I cradle it in my hand and head back toward the crowded streets of the current century.

LE CUPCAKE
3€50

Caramel
Fleur de Sel
-
Salted Caramel

Fraise-Citron
-
Strawberry
Lemonade

1:45 PM

RUE Saint-Louis *en* L'ÎLE

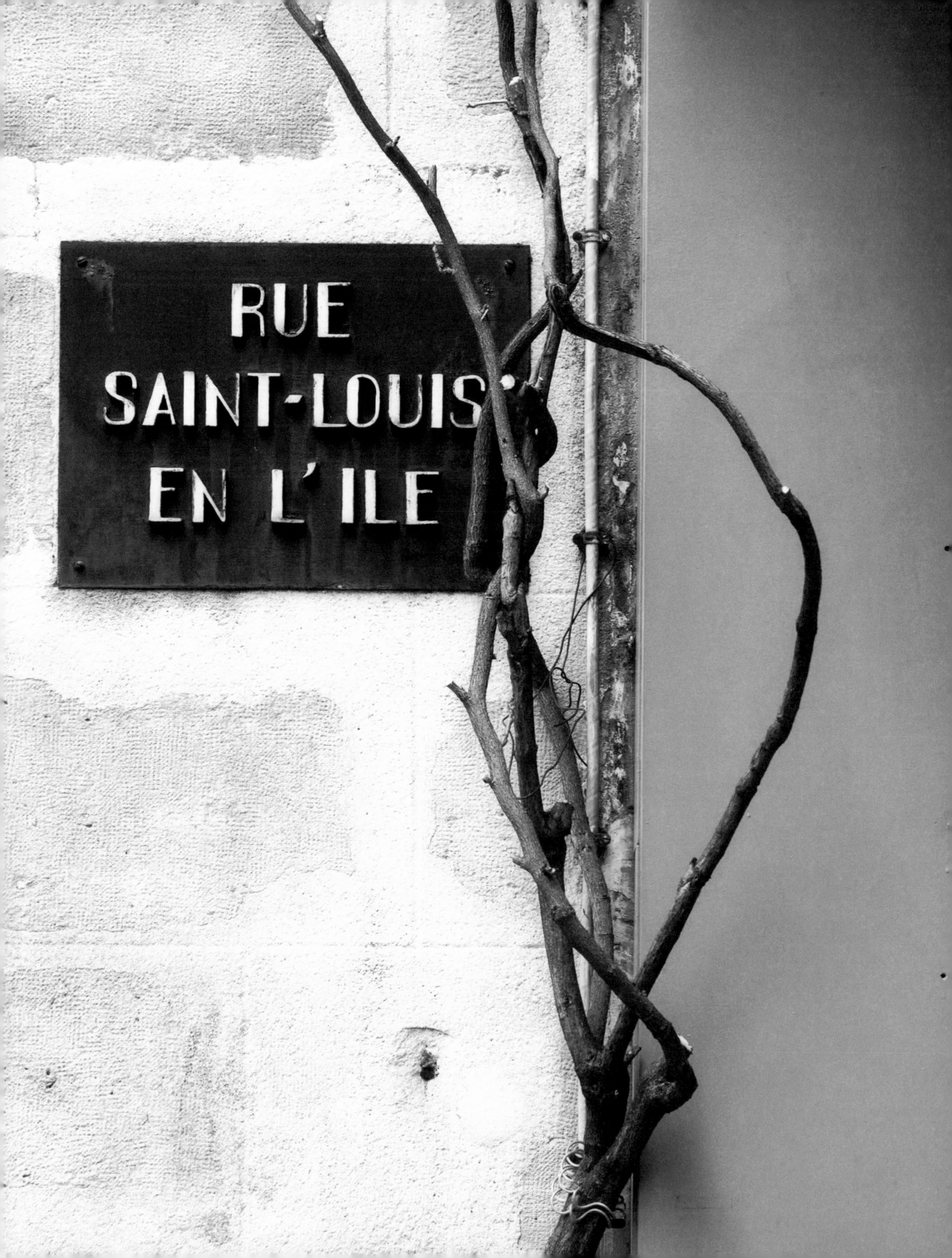
RUE
SAINT-LOUIS
EN L'ILE

I CROSS THE PONT SAINT-LOUIS, AND WADE INTO THE CONFLUENCE OF CROWDS FROM NOTRE DAME AND RUE JEAN DU BELLAY.

The few bites of cupcake took the edge off the hunger. I flow along with the crowd down Rue Saint-Louis en l'Île, the only interior street on the Île Saint-Louis.

The river of people wind down the street together, eddying into pools in front of shop windows for a moment, then flowing on again. Only the serious go inside. In my experience with the small shops in Paris, to enter is to buy. Unless you have a will of steel and a good grasp of the subtleties of the French language, you will end up buying something. I have neither, so I always stick to the street unless I mean business.

The crowd trickles past the heavy worn doors that lead to private courtyards and gardens, past gift shops and candy stores, past butcheries and florists (which are much the same in my case). A pair of fanny-sacked Americans spot my cupcake and ask where they could get one. I'm ashamed, so I feign having no English:

"Desolée, je suis Sainte Geneviève."

Confused, they squeeze out of the crowd and head down a narrow street that offers a glimpse of the open water and the bank beyond.

Because pedestrians routinely use the narrow street, almost no one drives on it. But the owner of the racing green convertible behind us obviously didn't get the memo. He honks his horn, like the street isn't for people, corralling the crowd onto the sidewalks.

I reach my destination just as the car and the crowd reaches me. I duck into the doorway of La Ferme Saint-Aubin, barely avoiding another cupcake malfunction. Cheese at last!

I step inside. Because when it comes to cheese, I do mean business.

The door pulls closed and the potent aromas of the cheese hit me. Pungent, volatile scents mix with the deep, sweet, earthy smells of alchemical milk. I'll pretty much try any cheese, but I have found that I prefer young goats and old cows. I don't like gray areas. No whiskey in my coffee please, no weak tea or brownies with ice cream. I hate most covers and all remixes. With cheeses, it's the same - I like strong, simply stated flavors.

Speaking of strong and simply stated, the shop owner is – well, I'm not going to give you the satisfaction of saying "handsome" – let's say *congenial*. Surprisingly young, with cropped brown hair and bright blue eyes. I say hello, suddenly embarrassed by what I will now choose not to write.

I avert my eyes to the perfect stacks of chèvre, hunks of hard cheeses and small wooden boxes of Camembert.

To stall for time I slowly intone, "I would like…"

Cheese shops are not unlike adult video stores. Row after row of subtle spins on the same intoxicating subject. The options make my heart race: Bloomy, washed, sweet, creamy, tangy, and shapely.

The cheesemonger grins. He knows.

He knows I'm a sad, twisted cheese junky. I stand absolutely still to hide my desire, but if I had a tail it would be wagging. Then I spot a perfect pyramide cendrée perched on a stack of crottins. The King of the Hill and his little soldiers, too. Oh, your majesty…

"…one pyramide please. And three of these crottins here, please." My hand unconsciously points, and smashes my cupcake into the glass.

Oh my God! What now? What if he doesn't give me any cheese?

He smiles and hands me a napkin. I apologize and thank him, wiping the glass.

"No no, it's for your fingers," he says.

I thank him again, looking down. As he wraps up my pyramide and the crottins (and a big ol' sexy hunk of 30-month comté), he smiles and wishes me a good day. Cheese in hand, I coast out the door.

I make my way toward the boulangerie for a baguette. Then I notice the beautiful old woman I had seen praying in Notre Dame.

She's moving at a moderate pace, and steps out of the street and onto the sidewalk underneath a stately clock that juts out from the stone building. She takes her time with the steps, entering a door that I've never noticed, and disappears inside.

I weave across the street toward the door, putting off the bakery for the moment. Pinching the remains of my pulverized cupcake between two fingers, I step up to the door and into some place new.

38 SAINT LOUIS

FROMAGE VIN

CHEESE
VACUUM
PACK

CIBOULIER
4.05 €

Deux-Sèvres

Chèvre cru

PYRAMIDE
CENDRÉ
6.05 € la pièce

DEUX SÈVRES

Chèvre cru

SAUVAGET
BLANC
4.70 €

LA TOUR
Fermier
Lait cru 1.35

QUAI D'ORLÉANS

Famules 12ʰ - 19ʰ

Tous nos plats sont faits "Maison"
Everything is home-made

Plat - Main Course 14€

Plat du Jour Today's Special 14€

Pavé de Saumon à la Plancha, purée
de pommes de terre à l'huile d'Olive

Entrée & Plat ou Plat & Dessert 18€

Entrée, Plat & Dessert 24€

Entrées

Salade de Roquette Arugola Salad
Soupe à l'Oignon, croutons & Parmesan
Onion soup, toasted bread & Parmesan

Librairie
Paris
et son
Patrimoine

Église Saint-Louis-en-L'ÎLE

WELL, CRAP. IT'S A CHURCH.

I have stumbled into a church with strong cheese and cupcake fingers. Tailing an old lady. Jesus is not pleased.

Worse, I'm mortified that I didn't know this church existed. How many times have I walked by this door and ignored it? In any city in America, this chapel would be a treasure, but here it's lost in the shadow of Notre Dame and Sainte-Chapelle and every other Big Name Church in the city.

If I were a monument, I would prefer to be on the b-list. These spots have become my favorite places in Paris. No bling, no fireworks, no crowds or history placards. No expectations, tickets or photo opportunities. No compulsion to do something, to photograph something, to remember something. This is just a place to be quiet. To surround yourself with something that lifts you up and lets your mind wander. The old woman lights a votive candle. Apparently, she feels the same way. I sneak a bite of what's left of my cupcake.

She pauses and looks at me. I give her a sheepish smile. Then I cross myself and take a seat in the last row of the church to stall for time.

I should just put my feet up and belch while I'm at it.

The lady turns toward the altar, approaches it, then genuflects next to a seat and lowers herself into it. She stares ahead. I sneak another bite. Watch how fast I can make this cupcake disappear. She may not even remember that I had it. And if she calls the churchwarden, there'll be no proof. Well, there's the cheese. But that's very French, so I'm more likely to get off with a warning.

Who is she? Why has she come to two churches today? I bet there will be more. But why? A tour, maybe? Dan Brown treasure hunt? Some kind of Catholic pub crawl?

It hits me. She lost someone. Perhaps a sister. Yes.

Her sister passed away and she promised to visit every church they went to together. Her younger sister, Mathilde. Some zealous priest excommunicated her in 1966 for leaving her husband and having a wild affair with a Tunisian man living in the Jewish Quarter. Her parents disowned her, of course, so they had to get married. In a desperate bid at citizenship, the Tunisian joined the Foreign Legion and returned to the sub-Sahara where he promptly died of Legionnaire's disease. Total tragedy.

Left all alone, Mathilde only had her sister to turn to. They would visit in secret places around the city where their parents wouldn't spot them. Many years later, when she died, she was denied a Christian burial. And now her sister secretly scatters the ashes in churches, three a day, twice a week, one thimble full in each church. Forget the love locks, *that's* an act of love and defiance.

That's my theory, anyway.

But where are the ashes? She's not scattering anything.

She sits motionless. When the light in the windows shifts, I see through the hem of her coat for a moment. It's empty. I realize in horror that this isn't Mathilde's sister; it's Mathilde herself. This is her ghost, unable to rest after the death of her lover, the loss of her family and the scorn of the church. Slowly she rises, half bows to the altar and pivots toward me. Our eyes meet and I see that it's all true.

I stand up, cross myself and head for the door a little too quickly.

Square du Vert Galant

I'VE PUT 10 BLOCKS BETWEEN THE CHURCH AND ME BEFORE I THINK ABOUT WHERE I AM GOING, AND REALIZE I FORGOT TO BUY THE BAGUETTE.

Have you ever tried to eat cheese without a cracker or bread? It gets trashy fast. I'm suddenly angry with the woman (and my imagination) for derailing me. Wandering around Paris for the sake of wandering is freeing. But wandering back and forth because you have a screw loose is a drag.

I spot a bistro across the street, Le Soleil d'Or, and a desperate idea seizes me. Someone is just standing up from their table to go, leaving behind a half-eaten omelette and an untouched basket of bread. While the waiter greets the table behind him with his back to me, I scoot past, and dump the basket of bread into the plastic bag with my cheese. I slink out, looking around like I need to pick a direction for my casual, not-stealing-anything stroll. I feel like a first-rate gangster. Godard would be proud.

I head toward the statue with the spoils of my raid in hand and my heart in my throat. I'll offer half to Good King Henry and then make penance for my crime by feeding the pigeons cheese and bread until they burst.

As I approach the verdigris statue of Henri IV on horseback, he smiles and dismounts.

"Hello, your highness," I say.

"Hello, my sweet. You look shaken."

"I've had an odd day. I stole some bread."

"In Paris, that's a cliché. Shall we go down to the square?"

"You mean the triangle?"

"Of course."

"And no funny business."

He escorts me down the long flight of steps that lead to the Square du Vert Galant. I'm not kidding about the funny business. Henry IV may have been an exemplary ruler, but he was a total skirt-chaser. The Vert Galant bagged many a babe, and this was his favorite spot. This was his make-out point. His Blueberry Hill.

In the center of the square is a small park with a flower garden. It is slightly elevated from the rest of the point, with a low railing that separates the space in two: book readers and pigeon-feeders above, and river gazers and randy lovers below. Only the railing and an unspoken agreement not to stare separate them from each other.

The King prefers the view from below.

Circumnavigating the main park, I stumble along the uneven cobblestones of the lower embankment, careful not to slip down the sharp slope to the water a few feet down. The weather is bordering on hot for the moment and the couples are out: flirting, drinking, laughing, kissing. We walk until we reach the very edge of the island, which juts into the water like the prow of a ship.

The couple about five feet away from us is, well, kind of going at it. Even for Paris, they're testing the limits.

Henry can sense my discomfort. "Oh, they're charming," he says.

"I suppose they're all charming. Or rather charmed, I think."

"What do you mean?"

"You cast a long shadow."

"I have nothing to do with it," he says.

One careless limb-toss and the lovers may career over the edge into the Seine.

"You know, this would never fly in America."

"Which part?" he asks.

"Any of it."

"Americans don't kiss?"

But I don't mean the kissing. I'm not uptight. I mean the rest of it. In America, every aspect of this square would be regulated or prohibited. There would be a safety rail, flat, rough cement walkways and ugly signs prohibiting alcohol and bare feet. Come to think of it, you probably wouldn't even be able to come down here.

I settle in near the lone weeping willow tree on the point. No, I don't do this metaphorically. It's just a good place to rest my back. But I bet many girls have cried under this tree over the centuries.

"It seems a lot of girls cry in Paris," I say, taking out the pyramide cendrée and spreading out the plastic bag in my lap.

"A lot of boys, too," he replies.

"Yes, but mostly the girls."

"Would you like to?" he asks.

I ignore the question. "This cheese is outstanding."

I use the crust of a baguette like a knife and slice into the pyramid of cheese. The bloomy rind is gray-black from vegetable ash, but the inside gleams like fresh snow. The texture is firm and barely crumbly, just soft enough to scoop. It's perfect.

The lovers have gone from charming abandon to outright moaning. I focus on the view, trying to contain my laughter. In the distance, the Pont des Arts shines in the sun, blemished only by the growing number of bicycle locks on its wire mesh.

Oh no, the disease is spreading!

I'm caught with my fingers (and a chunk of comté) in my mouth when a strong wind threatens to blow the bag out of my lap. I save it with a slap.

I take a triumphant bite and enjoy the sound of the waves. A short gasp from the park above breaks the spell. A group of tourists have just returned from their boat ride, and one of the women is trying to contain her shock after seeing the couple.

I notice the even spacing of all the people on the bridge. "It's funny how everyone knows to keep a certain distance," I say. "I wonder what that is."

"1.6 meters," says Henry without hesitation. "The length of a park bench."

I take this in. "Makes sense."

Behind me, the woman clicks her camera. I guess the shock has turned into something else. On the other side of the park, the next group is boarding the boat. The water sloshes back and forth between the hull and the shore and the sound is comforting. For a moment I think about taking a ride. Then I get a better idea.

I scarf a final bite of the pyramide and wrap up the other half for later.

"Gotta go."

"Alright. Until next time," Henry says.

I'd like to think that he is more than a little dismayed by my departure.

I leave him in his park with his amorous entourage. But I'm not heading up the steps to the street. I am staying down here. Around the edge of the point, the rough path continues along the Seine underneath the Pont Neuf. The monstrous stone masks that line the bridge peer down at me as I cross the threshold into the shadow and the long, wide, cobblestone quay beyond.

4:45 PM

les
Bateliers

MY HEAD IS LOOPY. IS IT THE BREAD? THE PHEROMONES? A DAY WITHOUT SLEEP, PERHAPS?

Sleep deprivation always makes me feel like a stoner who doesn't realize how obvious her observations are:

Water... it's just. It's just ... so primal. We... are... water. A strong, slow emphasis on the last word, a stare into the hapless listener's bloodshot eyes, and a bid for understanding. *You know, man?*

But, there's a simple truth to the lure of the water. This quay is the border between the reality of "here" and the possibility of "out there." I reach the first small boat moored to the island. It's a black batelier with super sexy white trim. A few deck chairs adorn the roof and a clean cabin can be made out through the portholes. Her name is Louise.

I want to own a boat. I want to hop on Louise, let her loose and escape.

Boats built this city. It was born from the river. To the Celtic tribes that first settled here, the river was everything - food, protection, travel, trade, and if all else failed, escape. Their cultural descendants are people who live their lives on boats like Louise.

The boat people have carried their cargo up and down the river for centuries. They live off of the river, and they live on it. I read that they have struggled to survive in the last few decades, and the number of boats has dwindled to almost nothing. They have become an endangered species.

I stare at Louise, thinking about the owners. From a crane in the back, a small rowboat can be lowered on a heavy, knotted rope. I imagine the intrepid captain in a storm, lowering his wife and children into the sea as the boat careens toward jagged rocks. They pull away as he takes one last puff of his pipe and goes down with the ship.

Don't ask me where this is - there are no jagged rocks in the Seine obviously. Just in my head. At this moment, the boat is still and serene and I wish I were on it.

At one point, the government was somehow forcing them to retire their boats because railroads and trucks were more efficient, but then the powers that be decided to subsidize the boat trade instead. That makes these boats a preserved cultural relic. I suppose the reality is not enticing, but the fantasy is overwhelming. I don't come to Paris expecting to fall in love in my beret and striped shirt, but if a boat captain asked me, I would so be onboard.

I bet I could pilot her. She's big but not so big that you would need navigational equipment. The SUV of the boat world. Just big enough.

Out on the river, a massive Freycinet barge shoves the water aside. It smells of diesel. That thing has navigational equipment. An 18-wheeler. It looks like it's carrying 300 tons of sand. He's a bully. Don't worry, I'll defend you, Louise.

Another 100 feet along the quay, a cluster of boats sways back and forth in the bully's wake. Each one is distinct. They are brightly painted - turquoise, red, white - and they have romantic names like Jolia, Daphné and Ark. Oh, I should go with Ark. Ark would never go down in a storm. But how could I leave Louise after all we've been through?

Looking up from this vantage at the steep walls and the buildings beyond, it strikes me that the island itself resembles a ship. For a long time, it has been it's own ark of sorts, for all manner of artists. Some practiced writing, some painting or dancing or sculpting. But on this boat, this little island, all of them practiced the art of escape.

It is the greatest of art forms.

MAISON
Berthillon

A NARROW STONE STAIRCASE LEADS BACK UP TO THE STREET, WHICH IS FLOODED WITH LATE AFTERNOON LIGHT.

The full sun on my face is bright enough, in fact, to conjure the illusion of summer. Never mind that I need to tighten my scarf against the wind, it's summer-ish for the moment. At any rate I'm warm enough to go to Berthillon for ice cream.

Unfortunately, to get there I need to walk back past the bistro where I pulled a Jean Valjean. I carefully time my passing with the street traffic to hide my face. Through the blur of vehicles, I glance sideways at the bistro, expecting someone to spot me and call the baguette-police. There he is, the waiter. My cheeks prickle and I walk a little faster.

I hear no shouting for the cops. I risk another glance, and of course he isn't looking at me. He's staring at the buildings across the water, wishing his shift away. I will live to repent, but one thing is clear: I would never make it in a Victor Hugo novel. I hurry to the Île Saint-Louis for my ice cream.

Once you hit the island, the Berthillon logo is everywhere. Seemingly every café serves it, and proudly displays the logo in their windows, giving the false impression that you've already arrived. But you haven't. There is only one original Maison Berthillon where they serve the fresh stuff, some of which is still made right upstairs.

It's hard to miss; it's the one with a line.

I hop on the end behind a group of three travelers in trench coats. It's an odd day for coats, either too hot or too cold. The two men have taken theirs off in the warmth of the sun, but the woman keeps hers tightly belted and positions herself in the growing shadow against the wall to compensate. They amuse themselves to pass the time, but they can't hide the anticipation just below the surface. It doesn't matter how old you are: ice cream makes you happy.

To an American like me, the demure, golf-ball-sized scoops can be a shock. We're trained to expect baseball- or, in amusement parks and on boardwalks, full softball-sized scoops. The arms race of food portions.

By contrast, Berthillon seems undersized. That is until you taste it. This is ice cream distilled to its purest and most potent. This ice cream isn't a pint of beer; it's an ounce of single-malt whiskey, and its value cannot be measured by its volume.

The threesome is close enough to see the menu now, and they've stopped joking. Selecting an ice cream flavor is serious business. The shorter man asks the woman for advice.

"What should I have?" he asks.

"One can always judge a creamery by its vanilla," she says.

"Perfect. Let's get vanilla," he says.

"I don't know, a bit boring, perhaps." She turns to the taller man. "What about you?"

He leans toward her. "Salted butter caramel. Anything but boring."

I'm convinced that at least two and possibly all three of them are going to end up in bed later.

As the line lengthens, tensions rise. Someone in the back asks what time it is, and there's a palpable fear about closing time. Hoarding instincts kick in as people crane their necks and shuffle their feet.

The woman reaches the counter and orders herself a caramel through the narrow curve of her mouth.

"Two," says the taller man.

"I'll take the nougat!" adds the short one, hoping to outdo his rival with a last-minute switch to a bold contrarian choice.

I'm secretly rooting for him as the victor. I love an underdog.

The woman and taller man stroll away with their caramels while Nougat pays and follows after them. He eyes his cone suspiciously. But after one test lick, his stance relaxes. He realizes there's no wrong choice here. The pure ice cream is dense, rich and impossibly creamy. No softballs needed; this is meant to be savored. And like a magic potion in a storybook, one drop is all it takes to work its spell on you.

I get a double caramel. I could be hit by a taxi tomorrow.

Salon de thé

Glaces & Sorbets

Patisseries

Petit déjeuner

Lait d'amande
ALMOND

Feuille de menthe
Mint

Chocolat au nougat

poire Bourdaloue
Poire & Lait d'amande

Caramel au gingembre
GINGER   CARAMEL

Marron Glacé
CHESTNUT WITH RHUM +0.3€

Vanille
Vanilla

Pain d'épices
Ginger bread

Spéculos

Caramel Nougatine

Strawberry Daïquiri
Daïquiri aux fraises & rhum

Nouveau cocktail exotiqu
Lo Batida do Brazil

Poire
Pear

Pêche
peach

Pêche de vigne
Vine peach

Ananas
Pineapple

Ananas rôti basilic frai
Roasted pineapple & fresh basi.

Fraise
Strawberry

Abricot
Apricot

Fruit de la passion
Passion fruit

Mirabelle
Cherry plum

7:45 PM

APÉRO

I STROLL TOWARD THE QUAY TO ENJOY THE LAST OF THE SUN.

The air is chilly but calm for the moment. It will be night soon, and I open my coat to absorb the last of the warmth for later.

Halfway through my caramel ice cream, the jet lag and the day finally catch up with me. My pace slows to a crawl until I give up and sit near the steps that lead to the water.

Below, a dinner boat pushes upriver, under the Pont de la Tournelle. The waves lap against the walkways, spilling over their small embankment in the unusually high water, and roll toward the stone wall beneath me. The bow of the ship reaches the bridge, and the engine echoes through the tunnel. Some of the passengers standing on the deck wave to me as they disappear under the arch. I imagine myself as I would want them to see me: the charming young lady with her ice cream by the Seine. In Paris, everyone is part of someone else's painting.

This is especially true at certain times of day. Apéro is cocktail hour and perfect for people-watching. A glass of wine would put me to sleep, but a cup of coffee followed by a glass of wine just might work. I head up the street to Café Saint-Régis again, looking for the perfect place to sit.

I have to wait for a few minutes, but a table opens up with a view of the restaurants on either side, the bridge, Notre Dame and the sun - perfect. The last patron left his newspaper at my table, and I skim the headlines: scandal, tragedy, thievery. The usual. I put the paper down and order my coffee. I feel more awake already, a Pavlovian response to the clinking of cups and the smell of ground beans.

Most of the others are drinking wine or beer. A very well-to-do woman next to me has a kir royal. She's wearing a satin scarf, a pair of Holly Golightly sunglasses and vintage boots. The distinguished gentleman next to her is talking politics while she checks her reflection in a compact. A small white dog rests by her feet. The dog is staring at the woman's scarf and holding back a yip. The man reaches down to pet the dog, which sends its tail wagging. He brushes a bit of dust off of his polished shoe, then returns his hand above the table to accentuate a point he's making about Hollande's folly.

The cigarette-smoking waiter from this morning is moving fast now, managing the throng of arrivals. He brings me a coffee and another for the young guy to my left. He is writing, but he has no journal, only a napkin. His shirt is pressed and rolled at the sleeves. The sun has intensified and we have both taken off our coats. He glances at me and smiles, gesturing to his coffee. Hey there, look what we have in common. I smile back but suddenly get the impression that he's writing nonsense to paint a picture for me. Nice try, stud.

Sure enough, his girlfriend comes over the bridge waving her arms. The guy stands up to greet her, a kiss on each cheek and then a third. Cad.

On every side now, Parisians and tourists are drinking and sunning themselves. The cocktails are probably too expensive, but the view is irresistible. We've all made a silent pact to ignore the cost, get tipsy together and watch day transition to night. When the air is still, the sun heats our faces and sleeves. But the clouds are moving faster now and the wind whips over the water across the tables. The weather at this time of year is mercurial, but it doesn't matter. We want to be outside, and the café provides red wool blankets on the benches. A few of the ladies have already spread the blankets over their laps. The men won't do it, of course; they pretend not to mind. But under the table, Young Guy is secretly rolling down his sleeves while nodding along to his girlfriend's story.

It's getting chilly. I put my hand around my coffee but it has lost most of its heat. Out of fear of falling asleep too soon, I suck it down in one gulp and order a Bordeaux.

The amber sun approaches the roof of Notre Dame, turning it into a black shadow. In the apartments that line the Île Saint-Louis, lights are coming on. The street lamps are still unlit, except by the light of the sun itself. It aims low now, cutting across the lamps along the bridge and casting long dark lines across a few of the patrons' faces. The dog has curled up to nap with its body in the sun and its face just inside the shadow. The white noise of 20 simultaneous conversations is punctuated by glasses being placed, toasted and bussed.

We are sun worshippers, water gazers, ushers of night on the crest of something at once routine and extraordinary. In this moment, anything can happen. Yet we are content to do nothing. Together, we enjoy the last warmth of the day and the first drink of the night.

8:30 PM

PONT de la Tournelle

THE SUN HAS ALREADY DIPPED BELOW NOTRE DAME BY THE TIME I'VE PAID AND LEFT.

The shadows have taken the street, so I head to the river for the best view of the setting sun. On the water, a tour boat pulls ahead, threatening to beat me to the perfect vantage point for sunset.

Race!

I dash around a group of high school students and under the arm of their teacher, who is pointing up at the south rose window of the church. The sightseers on the boat shoot a volley of camera snaps at me as I leap over a puddle. They couldn't possibly be shooting that beautiful cathedral behind me bathed in beautiful light. I'm sure they're shooting me competing in the 2014 Paris Puddle Leap.

It's not easy being this talented. The paparazzi never leave you alone.

Finish line! I beat the boat to the bridge by a nose. Let those German judges contest the results all they want. The sun throws its enormous spotlight on me as the crowds go wild. Victory is mine.

The lengthening shadows of the Left Bank reach toward the water. Already, the streets across the river are dark, and pedestrians and bikers have tightened their scarves and zipped their coats. But the sunlight still sparkles on most of the river, and bounces back up onto stone facades. I walk out to the center of the bridge where the light is most intense.

On the quay, five friends pour some wine into plastic cups and lean back on their elbows. Two of them, a young couple, are arguing. She pulls her hand from his in a gesture of disdain. The other three cheer on the show.

They're playing out a well-worn story. I doubt her anger was sincere; but even if it was, she'll get her storybook ending. A romance may end triumphantly or tragically, but it won't be boring. Not in this place.

This is where Hemingway fished. Where Scott wrestled Zelda. Where Stein kissed Toklas. Where Baudelaire glowered at a dress. And we are all part of it. Part of the same story.

Let your relationship fizzle out in Brooklyn or Sacramento. In Paris, the boy grabs the girl's hand, confesses his love, and kisses her. He has no choice. The story is already written.

The sun grows confident in the last moments before its final fall. The shadows climb the buildings behind me like ivy. The water turns dark green as the sun shrinks down into the chimneys until it's gone. The last rays illuminate the glass in the lamp heads above me before the earth revolves the city into twilight.

la Seine

THE SKY AT THE FAR END OF THE CITY IS ALREADY TURNING INDIGO.

The five friends on the quay exchange kisses and calls of "ciao" and "à bientôt," then head in separate directions. The three hecklers bound up the steps while the girl takes her guy by the arm and the wine bottle by the neck. They stumble along the river path, past dear old Louise and the other bateliers, orbiting each other in a clumsy dance.

Up on the street, a woman in black cigarette pants bicycles past me. Her headlamp flickers on and off, powered by the turning wheels. I wonder who she is, and where she's headed. Maybe somewhere, maybe nowhere, like me. Cities are anonymous places, and in a foreign country, the barriers are almost absolute. It's usually liberating. But right now, as I watch people gather into smaller and smaller groups, gabbing on their way to drinks and dinner, I'm not so sure.

When did I last eat? I need to find something soon. I don't have enough money for anything extravagant. That place at Place Dauphine, La Rose de France, may be alright. Or Au Fin Gourmet on the Île Saint-Louis. The bistros are fine but boring. So is sitting alone. Maybe a sandwich to go.

On the Pont Neuf, a group of beautifully dressed Brazilians are taking selfies with the Eiffel Tower in the background. They ask me to take a picture of them all together, which of course I'm happy to do.

I know exactly what they want. It's a picture I never take myself, but know very well. I wait for the tower's lighthouse beacons to arc past the lens and snap the photo. Fortunately they give no duck lips or gang signs - that would have been disappointing. Their camel coats, tasteful dresses and sleek heels tell a different story, the one that I prefer to write for them. The girl with the ponytail smiles and looks at the image. The tower is glittering like a prom girl in a sequined dress: sexy, flamboyant and tacky.

The arc of the light is both beautiful and a little creepy. Like the dread eye of Sauron. But they love it and that's what matters.

They are all so kind as they leave that I almost want to chase after them like a puppy. But I don't have the strength to keep up with the Brazilians tonight. I don't even have the energy to imagine their adventures. I decide to go for one more stroll down by the water instead. Tomorrow I will leave these islands, and head to the Left Bank or Montmartre maybe, but I want to see the boats at night one more time.

As I make my way toward the steps. I peer into restaurant windows. Couples (always couples!) gaze at each other in the isolated light of lamps and candles. They play it cool; they play hard to get; they play with words.

Down by the water, someone is strumming guitar. I don't know the song, mercifully. I couldn't take Radiohead right now. As I approach, I smell pot in the cold air. The guitarist is sitting with a few friends, and they're all very baked and very happy.

The uneven cobblestones by the water are harder to navigate in the dark. Would the stoners have enough sense to fish me out if I fell in? Or would they just play Radiohead while I drowned?

Underneath the Pont des Arts, the wood and metal lattices create patterns and shadows that shift against the black water. A girl straddles a boy on a bench and is kissing him hard. She shifts toward him, and her leg knocks over a bottle from the bench next to them. They don't seem to care.

12:00 AM

MINUIT

THIS EMPTY NIGHT IS AN ESCAPE.

The streets fall asleep, one by one. The people wander off, round corners and disappear, leaving the stone and light all to me. I watched Paris wake up, and I will watch it fall asleep.

Groups of friends say goodnight, lovers walk home, restaurants and bars turn out the lights. Only the poets and philosophers roam the streets now. Too cliché? Maybe. But we all feel we are poets when we're alone in the dark.

A waiter closes down the café, stacking the chairs up, putting the remaining cups and dishes away. A friend keeps him company at the bar. The waiter sweeps the cigarette butts out to the street and into the gutter. In a few more hours, the washing outlets will again turn on and carry them away to the sewer. He pulls the chairs inside, closes the gate down halfway across the storefront, and turns off the lights. Up above, a light comes on in one of the balcony apartments, and a woman leans out of the window to light a cigarette.

City of Light. The name rings true when you're in the middle of a bridge, lights all around you with rows of illuminated facades in the distance. Like the rest of Paris, the nickname dates back farther than you would guess, to the Age of Enlightenment. It's the illumination of your mind that matters. The light is inside.

Off the busy thoroughfares, the traffic fades to a faint whisper, indiscernible from the wind and the river. On many streets, even the wind dies down to a breeze.

As I walk under a row of street lamps, I watch my shadow stretch out ahead of me farther and farther until it fades in the light of the next lamp. It happens again. Reach, fade. Reach, fade. The respiration of thought. I am in the light but I am not enlightened. I am alone, on an island. I'm walking down a path that leads toward myself.

My solitude is interrupted by someone walking toward me in the other direction. As he passes, we share the street for a moment, each feeling the other's presence. We exchange a glance, that mixture of hope and danger, and then we pass. I reclaim the street for myself. He heads toward my past, and I head toward his.

Dear city, your past is my future.

HÔTEL
DES
2 ÎLES

RUE
LE REGRATTIER

FIN

ACKNOWLEDGEMENTS

We'd like to thank all of our family, friends and fans for their unwavering support over the past five years. Your enthusiam and willingness to come along for the ride is what has kept us going.

Special thanks to Amy Feezor for her fab editing skills and late night chats in our apartment in the Passage du Grand Cerf. To Sarah Schlow - the most helpful beta reader ever - for her insights and suggestions. To Rachel Weber for her keen eye and willingness to talk us through many iterations of the project. To Jeri Gottlieb and Jason Gottlieb for the good advice and great meals - all of which were necessary to our process. To our art director, Marissa Rivera for her exquisite taste.

And a very special thanks to Ann Youtz and Les Youtz. We could fill another book cataloguing our gratitude and the ways in which you've supported us and helped us move forward despite overwhelming odds. Thank you for taking care of the boys and running our shops while we traveled. For often putting our needs before your own. And for believing in our vision for this project and so many others.